OLMO
and the Blue Butterfly

by Alma Flor Ada

illustrated by Viví Escrivá

translated by Kathryn Corbett

For Daniel Antonio
Welcome to the planet!

Requests for permission to make copies of any part of the work
should be mailed to: Permissions Department, Harcourt Brace & Company,
6277 Sea Harbor Drive, Orlando, Florida 32887-6777.

HARCOURT BRACE and Quill Design is a registered trademark of
Harcourt Brace & Company.

Grateful acknowledgment is made to Laredo Publishing Company, Inc. for
permission to reprint *Olmo and the Blue Butterfly* by Alma Flor Ada, illustrated
by Viví Escrivá. Copyright © 1993 by Laredo Publishing Co., Inc. Originally
published in Spanish under the title *Olmo y la mariposa azul*.

Printed in the United States of America

ISBN 0-15-307394-2

1 2 3 4 5 6 7 8 9 10   073   99 98 97 96

OLMO
and the Blue Butterfly

by Alma Flor Ada

illustrated by Viví Escrivá

translated by Kathryn Corbett

HARCOURT BRACE & COMPANY
Orlando   Atlanta   Austin   Boston   San Francisco   Chicago   Dallas   New York
Toronto   London

Olmo, sit up
and rub your eyes.

Look, a blue butterfly!
What a surprise!

Olmo, jump up.
Away you go!

Follow the butterfly high and low.

Hop on a scooter.
Away you go!

Follow the butterfly high and low.

Ride on a skateboard.
Away you go!

Follow the butterfly high and low.

Jump on a bike.
Away you go!

Follow the butterfly high and low.

Ride on a motorbike.
Away you go!

Follow the butterfly high and low.

Hop on a streetcar.
Away you go!

Follow the butterfly high and low.

Jump in a boat.
Away you go!

Follow the butterfly high and low.

Fly an airplane.
Away you go!

Follow the butterfly high and low.

Fly a chopper.
Away you go!

Follow the butterfly high and low.

Ride in a rocket.
Away you go!

Follow the butterfly high and low.

It's always with you
wherever you go.

Follow the butterfly high and low.